Graveyard

Underground Poetry

Maria De Jesus Alvarado

BookLeaf Publishing

India | USA | UK

Copyright © Maria De Jesus Alvarado
All Rights Reserved.

This book has been self-published with all reasonable efforts taken to make the material error-free by the author. No part of this book shall be used, reproduced in any manner whatsoever without written permission from the author, except in the case of brief quotations embodied in critical articles and reviews.

The Author of this book is solely responsible and liable for its content including but not limited to the views, representations, descriptions, statements, information, opinions, and references ["Content"]. The Content of this book shall not constitute or be construed or deemed to reflect the opinion or expression of the Publisher or Editor. Neither the Publisher nor Editor endorse or approve the Content of this book or guarantee the reliability, accuracy, or completeness of the Content published herein and do not make any representations or warranties of any kind, express or implied, including but not limited to the implied warranties of merchantability, fitness for a particular purpose.

The Publisher and Editor shall not be liable whatsoever...

Made with ❤ on the BookLeaf Publishing Platform
www.bookleafpub.in
www.bookleafpub.com

Dedication

To all who have *inspired* me and those that can **relate**.

Preface

When life throws me lemons, I write poetry...

Acknowledgements

I would like to thank
Hector, Andy, Marie, and Jeff
for being in my corner.
I appreciate the support and love
from my family and friends.

Me

Read my poetry.
Let my words
captivate your curiosity,
not my avatar!

My photograph
is a snap shot
of an emotion
set in motion
by my composition...

I'm not interested
in an illicit
proposition,
even if the content
is explicit!

*If you can't
perceive my poetry,
how can you presume
to understand
ME?*

*If you can't be absorbed
by my verses,
you can't possibly
be interested in
ME!*

*You think a rose
will impress me
and win you my favor?*

*If you can't adore
my prose,
how can you propose
to love
ME?*

You'll never taste

*the flavor
of my parted lips...*

*You'll never sway
the rhythm of my hips
or inspire my pen!*

I am my poetry!

Seek me through my words!

*Only then can you recognize
the real me, enough
to love
or hate
ME!!!!*

</3

At First Glance

I never stood a chance.
The light in your eyes
drew me in at first glance!
You had me without ever even asking.

That smile...
God, that smile
was worth unmasking!

Your touch made me feel juvenile.
Your kisses brought out the woman in me
I hadn't felt in a while...

I never stood a chance...

I put down my pen.
I wanted to feel something different from this pain!
I left unfinished poetry.
I had so much more to gain.

I gave myself to you
with open eyes,
an open mind,
and an open heart.

We intertwined our bodies
without bind.

My heart and mind for once agreed!
They let you in at record speed...

It all felt like a beautiful dream...
A pivotal moment in my life.

I never stood a chance!
I never stood a chance, did I?

I didn't stand a chance
next to her white, creamy skin.

Her unparalleled beauty
had me beat...

The dream became,
oh, so grim!

I was left unarmed

in the middle of the broken
pieces of my wall.

I couldn't lift myself up; I didn't want to...

I picked up my pen
to finish the poetry
I had left undone.

The end was much more painful
than the start...

The joy was gone...

I felt so much pain for being numb!

I felt so dumb for thinking
that I ever stood a chance...

Her daring style and youth
were too much competition
for a woman unwilling to compete!

I didn't stand a chance
against her erotic curves
and flowing hair...

They were all too perfect
to the point of being unfair...

7

I'm not blind...

I didn't stand a chance against anyone
because I NEVER stood a chance
with you!

</3

Tempted

I can't think my
world is upside down.
I've tried meditation,
but silence is too loud!
I can't feel anything else
other than this pain.
I've drank myself to sleep
and cried myself awake.
I can't write.
Trying to find inspiration
in all the wrong songs.
The sad lyrics
are too happy
for my broken heart.
I can't think
I can't feel
I can't write
the darkness
is not letting in the light!
I've allured death.

It has a grip on me,
but she finds pleasure
in the torture
of life.
I'm trapped.
I haven't attempted,
but I'm tempted.
I must go on
for what?
I have no more
possibilities
I'm at a dead end.
Ironic isn't it?!
An end without death!

</3

Kill or Be Killed

They say
the past is the past.
I'm to leave it behind.
But when the past is on repeat,
how do you overcome?
There is no way around it;
I'll RIDE through it!

I'm composed of:
pain,
smiles,
past,
present,
highs,
and lows.
Like a great symphony goes!

As my future unfolds,

I hold
those painful threads
that keep me strong.
I hold onto
those joyful memories
that lift me up.

It only stings
as the needle
breaks the skin...

They say
the past is the past.
In order to live,
I must leave it where it belongs
and not let it influence
what is to come...
Otherwise, I'm adding weight
to an already heavy cross...

Every artist paints
a bloody Christ...
A crown of thorns
digging into his flesh

to remind us
of what should've been forgotten?

Sometimes our sorrows
are the best
part of our lives...
Sometimes our death
is more important
than our life!
Pain has more depth
more meaning.
Tears have more strength
than a smile;
they tear,
unite,
and mend!

I'm my past.
I'm my hurt.
I'm my darkness
and my light...

I don't need a tissue.
I don't need pity!

My agony is not the issue.
You just don't understand
that to live,
you don't have to leave!
To rebuild,
you must allow
breakdown.
You don't have to use
all the broken pieces
to be whole...

As long as I have my pen
and my paper,
I will write myself right!
I will cry myself back strong!

In a kill
or be killed world,
I am a Samurai!!!!

</3

Us

I loved
our daily interactions.
Your weird
imitation of me
that always made me smile

I loved your reaction
to my playful insults.
(yeah, not everyone will get that).

But that's why I loved
what we had
because it was OURS!

People have their inside jokes,
and so did we.

But we also had this "inside" love
that NOBODY could see!

Suddenly
I get less
and less
and less
of this...

I'm afraid...

I am petrified
that "US"
will become "ME."

Me... alone

Me all over again!

me, Me, ME LONGING
for a man
that loved the "HIM"
more than the "US."

Me wanting
the man
that would rather
be alone
than to share
one minute

more
with me...

I'll be inside out
looking for
"YOU."

Wondering what I did wrong
to lose the "HIM"
that made
"US."

</3

Ride or Die

I was your ride or die
until time revealed
what you tried to hide...

You disguised
your excuses
with reason...

Each step you took
was in the direction
of treason!

Every word you said
added a bar to my prison!

I was your ride or die
until I ran out of reasons
to believe in your lies!

There are too many

unanswered "Whys."

But why do "whys" matter
when "What"
is an act
I can't ignore?!

You tore
my heart;
I can't handle more!

I was your ride or die...

I resent my fat
I resent my ugly
I resent the fact
that because of it,
you couldn't love me!!!

I was your ride or die!
Today I wish for the latter
because without my rider,
what else can matter?

I was your ride or die...
Now I will ride alone,
but I know I will see you

at every passing sign
on the road...

I will feel you
in the wind...

I will love you, baby,
until the very end!

</3

Unforgiving Pain

I have overcome the pain.
So I thought
until that song is played again.
I find a knot building up in my throat
as I skip through the notes.
I can't fast forward the memory.
It's dug in...
At this point,
I can't retreat!
The song isn't playing,
but my suffering is on repeat!
I don't understand why because
I'm out of love with him...
Why can't I fall out of the hurt?
I guess pain stays
long after
love is gone!!!

</3

Unavailing

You wanted her so bad
you were willing to break my heart.
I loved you enough to let you.

I am with the man I wanted.
A man that never wanted me!

None of it works...

Being with someone YOU love
does not work.
Being with someone who LOVES you
does not work.

LOVE requires PERFECT timing
and we are either early
or too late.

</3

Love at First Smile

Since I met you,
I promised myself
that you were just for fun.
I started leaving you,
from the first meeting.
I started to forget you,
from the first memory.

Years later
I didn't leave you,
I didn't forget you.
Even if I want to, I can't.
I've fallen in love with you.
I can't help it!
From the first encounter,
your lips hadn't kissed me.
Your hands hadn't touched me,
but your smile found mine.
Since then I can't conceive
a single moment without you.

It hurts me to love you,
but I'm happily suffering!

</3

Friend Zone

The outcome is clear.
I do not know if I should
continue to wait
for the expiration date.
I do not know if it is far.
I do not know if it is near.

I am afraid...
I am afraid to quit too soon
or wait too long.
Should I let you go
a little at a time?

Every day...
Every day I smile
on my way over
and cry on my drive back.
Every day as I kiss you hello
and hold you,
I bid you goodbye

It leaves me feeling so alone,
torn up inside.
I keep coming for hope,
hoping that you may have
a change of heart
and you will love me.
Love me as I've begun,
but as I know
you can't see past your eyes,
such is my luck

I try to help you heal,
even if you are
for someone else to have.

That time is finally here,
and it hurts so bad to hear.

I am left torn again.
What should I adhere to?
Everyone has something to say.
A piece of advice,
a story that may sway,
but at the end of the day
I am left alone
a decision

I must make on my own.

Should I let you go
or stay
in the friend zone?

</3

He Will Miss Me

He is going to miss me
when I am gone.
He does not realize
how many aspects of his life I fill.
He is going to miss me
when he wants to drink beer
and eat unhealthy food.
His perfect girl won't want to break the diet.
Because her body is all she has,
and perfection comes at a high price.
He is going to miss me
when he wants to feel something real,
and all he has are the kisses he bought.
He will miss me
when he is in Mexico and he sees some trenzas
and listens to the songs we always requested.
He will miss me
when he no longer has someone
to make him smile.
He will miss me

with a single thought
that will hit him
long after I am gone.

Note: I will leave traces of myself for you to find.

</3

Unrequited

I see the women you like,
and I am not it.
I am not your packaged deal.
I am just the woman
that is here.
I am too afraid
to accept it.
I like the illusion
that you care
and that I mean
something to you
regardless of my imperfections.
But I make you sick.
You look at the images that fit
your needs and ignite your desire
since I can't start
only put out the fire.

</3

I Will See You In My Dreams

My mother passed away,
but I am not in pain.
Before you judge me,
let me explain.

I lost my mother.
I shed my tears
long before this day.
I can't even recall
the last embrace.

I never got to ask
the question
that burns inside
my chest.

I was always too afraid
that the answer
would cause more damage

than to wonder.

Life is a race,
and death caught up.

I stand before
an open casket
wearing a black dress.
She looks so different...
Finally seems to rest.
Wearing black
now seemed unfit.

I did not get up to speak.
Whatever memories,
whatever words
are hers and mine to keep.

I did not pray
for one more day.
It seemed unfair
to wish to prolong distress.

I just sat there
and did not even listen
to what was said.

All I know is that
time went by so slowly,
yet this moment
came by so fast.

As they lowered her
into the ground,
I felt a sense of relief.
She was no longer bound.
Nothing; no one can hurt her now.

I lost my mother;
I shed my tears
long before this day.
But I never
bid goodbye to Momma,
not in life and not in death.

</3

Longing

I convinced myself
that you stayed
because you wanted
to be with me.

I stayed too
believing that love
swayed you
even though you never
said it
because actions
speak LOUDER
than words.

But you have been looking
in all sorts of places.
Your eyes are set
on someone other than me;
you just have not found
my replacement...

yet!

I should leave
but, I stay.
I want to see it through.
I want you
to face my pain.

I know
what people will say,
but I will be okay.
Nothing has ever gone
my way;
I know how to lose,
and the only thing
I have lost today
was this blindfold.

When you find
that I hold you a little closer,
I am simply holding you
the way you wish to hold her.

</3

Loss

You are not here.
I wake up every morning hoping,
and every morning hope dies.
You can't hear my cries;
you can't see my tears.
You go on thinking
I do not give a damn!

You are not here,
and I fell into a deadly depression.
I did not get up;
I have been down for a long time,
but I had three reasons not to give up.

I have not been the same
ever since you left.

It is hard to assume this loss;
it is unbearable.
I have not moved yet;
I am lost.
I do not know where you are,
yet I am told you await me.
Where?!
Tell me where!
I will run to you!

I reached out,
but you were out of reach.
You put up a wall
that I could not breach.
I have not been able to be myself.
I lost a side of me
I will never get back.
Some breakage is irreparable.

You may be able to replace me,
but you are irreplaceable.

</3

Empath

Suddenly
I am overcome
by an inexplicable
sadness.

(Can't speak of it.)
(It would be misconstrued as madness.)

My light
gets dimmed
almost
to complete
darkness...

I do not understand
how emptiness can be so full,
leaving no room.
I do not understand
how silence can be
so deafening.

I play a happy tune,
but it buries me
deeper into gloom!

I surround myself
with company,
but I have gotten
so good at hiding,
that they can't see
the storm inside of me...

(The best place to hide is in plain sight.)

Fake it until you make it
does not work...
I have been faking all my life!

I may be here,
but I am merely passing by!
A victory contested by some...
the misconception.
Others call it depression...
another misapprehension.

(Is anybody paying attention?)

I DO NOT WANT TO BE ATTUNED!

Knowledge is NOT power!
Realization is demolishing!

I do not have demons
inside of me
that I am fighting!!
They are all around.
You can easily spot them...
they are inhumane!
Creating "masterpieces"
with their atrocities.

I am not suicidal!
I do not want to be part of a world
that only pretends to function
because reality requires action!
I want reprisal.
I do not want to be part of a world
where evil
is entertaining
and people take pleasure
in destruction!
Demanding better
but refusing to be better!
The world is just a place

filled with hatred...

I AM NOT DEPRESSED!

I am not depressed...
I am disappointed!!!!

</3

Pedestal

I have elevated you
so high
that when this
is over,
I will be the one
they criticize.

They will never know
what pain you caused.
The torment
in every tear
that I have ever cried.

How alone I really am.

No one will ever know
that you were less
than a perfect man.

I talked you up

because I truly believed
that was who you were.

42

I did not realize
that version
was only for her...

</3

Off Beat

Sitting at home
sipping coffee
while looking for a song
that speaks to me...

When did everything
turn to nothing?

Time is off beat,
making the pain increase!

The music doesn't matter.
I can't hear the lyrics;
I can't feel the notes.
The noise
of my heart breaking
drowns everything
except for me...

You took over my mind!

I'm looking for a distraction,
but when you left,
you left nothing
other than destruction!

Sitting at home
sipping coffee
while looking for a song
that speaks to me,
I started writing
to you...
Words you'll never hear,
poems you'll never read,
pain you'll never feel,
tears you'll never see

Tears that drowned EVERYTHING
and spared me...

</3

Strapless Dress

Strapless dress,
no restraints,
no rips,
no blood stains.

I did not get to wear it.

When I bought it,
I was so happy.
It was a perfect fit!

I was daydreaming
of where he'd take me,
and after a fabulous night,
he'd take me.

He broke me.
My face was more purple
than my strapless dress.
He beat me senseless;

since then, I bleed different
breathe different.

I looked in the mirror
and did not recognize
who I'd become—
a feeble woman
undermined by a man.

You see, I loved him,
and it was my fault;
I made him mad,
and an angry man
can't control his fury.

If you ever encounter this,
you must move out of reach in a hurry;
you must be faster than his hands.

The aftermath is not pretty.

Never met a whole lotta women,
whole women.

My mother taught me
that silence is golden.
That after a beating

comes the holding,
and after the storm
there is a calm.
She was not wrong,
but it "cost" a lot of harm.

He gripped my arm
begged me to stay.
He promised he would never
lay a hand on me this way;
he would only touch me with tenderness.

I believed him,
it was like a honeymoon
all over again.
It felt so good to feel so good.

Before my bruises could disappear,
I was addicted to this euphoria.

As time progressed,
I took more of his fists
and less and less of his kisses.

His mood would change,
like the seasons.
I wasn't fast enough

to get out of the way—
my mistake.

Silence is golden, mother would say.
Her words stuck in my head
like a broken record playing over and over again.
I do not know what hit harder—
his punches or her words
both were binding.

Either way, I ended up bleeding.

I heeded a lesson she could not learn to teach it:
leaving is not betrayal and certainly not easy.

One day he hit me so hard
I got my senses back.

I took the hit
wore the bruise like a badge.
I did not hide,
I did not keep quiet.
The days of being submissive
were behind me.

I faced his aggression,
although he overpowered me,

he had no power over me.
I walked away, never to return.

The next day
I wore the strapless dress
with no restraints,
no rips,
no blood stains.
There was a reason I did not wear it that day.
It fit better today than yesterday!

</3

Goodbye My Love

I have been fighting back tears all day!
I have to go on
pushing through the pieces
of my broken heart
to find the beating one!!
I have no more excuses;
you've taken away so much
that there is nothing left.
My feelings are distorted,
but one remains clear:
I no longer feel fear.
My tears will soon catch up to my pain.
For now, I have to maintain my strength!
I'll face it alone.
I've done it before.
I'll do it again!
I don't have the luxury
to lay down and die over a man!
I never thought
I'd have to go on without you.

It's not a crime, but it feels like murder.
It's tough to face the truth,
but wishing doesn't get you what you want,
and faith doesn't help you push through!
You opened the world to me
and left me alone in it.
I am no martyr;
I won't deny my pain;
I'll hurt through it,
but I'll destroy any thought of you after today!
I won't retrace a single step.
I know you can replace me.
But trust me when I say
there will be a day
you'd wish it wasn't this way.
You'll feel the emptiness
my absence has left,
but it will be too goddamn late!
I've left more important people behind,
and I still go on
because you don't know strength
until pain hits you hard,
leaves you for dead,
and you get the fuck back up!

</3

The End

I can see myself dying.
Too many endings
for me to bear.

It's poetic justice
for my end to be this way.

I can feel myself
mourning my life
more than my death.

With tearful eyes,
a broken heart,
and a soulless body,
I utter the names
of those whom I love.

With my last breath,
I say an unheard
"Goodbye."

I'm mourning
the inevitable loss of time
we spent apart.

Life was worthless
when I lost you.

My grand finale
is as I began...

Nothing but a painful,
lonely cry!

I didn't leave
an unsaid
"I LOVE YOU"

nor an unfought fight.

But if, with time,
you come to miss me,
you'll find pieces of my heart
in the poetry
I've left behind.

I'm slipping into a sleep

I've long longed for.

It feels surprisingly good
for being so painful.

There is no light...
Much like my life.

Darkness, I never left you,
and I see, you never left me.

</3

www.ingramcontent.com/pod-product-compliance
Lightning Source LLC
Chambersburg PA
CBHW061716130726
47996CB00006B/2349